Starter Mothers

poems by

Pamela Wax

Finishing Line Press
Georgetown, Kentucky

Starter Mothers

ACKNOWLEDGMENTS

Thanks to the editors of the publications in which the following poems first
appeared, sometimes in slightly different versions:

Artemis Journal—"The Royal We"
Bryant Literary Review—"Cousin J."
The Dewdrop—"Capricorn Loses His Star"
The Year of Mourning, CCAR Press—"Dropping Stones from the Heart"
Connecticut River Review—"The Little Prince Said It First"
DASH Literary Journal—"Eve Shelters in Place"
Relief: A Journal of Art and Faith—"The Angel Came to You as Picasso"
Green Ink Poetry—"Bird in Captivity"
Naugatuck River Review—"Dear Fertility"
Oberon Poetry Magazine—"Starter Mothers"
Passengers Journal—"Elegy for the Lady on Liberty Island"
Penmen Review—"Conjuring Bread from the Earth"
Pensive Journal—"Over the Ocean"
Platform Review—"A New Song"
Reservoir Road Literary Review—"And Sora Laughed"
Steam Ticket Journal—"The Time Turner, as Seen on Facebook"
Voices de la Luna—"The Hostess," "Being Woman as Superpower"

Publisher: Leah Huete de Maines
Editor: Christen Kincaid
Cover Art: Susan Musinsky and Travis Denton
Author Photo: Nick Mantello
Cover Design: Travis Denton

Order online: www.finishinglinepress.com
also available on amazon.com

Author inquiries and mail orders:
Finishing Line Press
PO Box 1626
Georgetown, Kentucky 40324
USA

Table of Contents

Extinction is the rule. Survival is the exception.
  —*Carl Sagan*

Dear Fertility

What have you done with my eggs,
the ones that dropped inchoate
and bloody into the toilet
for forty-nine years?
Had you fooled my birth control du jour,
been prankster enough
to pull one over God and me,
I might have been eye candy
at Stop & Shop's check-out, crowning
the cover of *The Enquirer*, a miracle
mother at sixty.

Instead, I was only Dr. D.'s private
wonder. I'd be lying if I didn't tell you
I almost wish there'd been a deus ex
machina flying from the wings
to explain your longevity—how
I'd missed my true calling, or maybe

that my child would have been a *lamed-vavnik*,
one of the thirty-six in a generation
who hold up the world like Malala
and Greta, Emma, and Darnella,
and it's all my fault there's no messiah.

Perhaps I botched the plot line
through my intransigence, my only
pregnancy aborted by choice,
so you've shadowed me ever since,
a loyal temptress, hanging on
for a different ending. Maybe

you decided to keep me company
from the beginning, the first page
of our memoir when I was eleven,
away at camp, and my father waxed
poetic about my womanness.

Or maybe you liked how my mother
never officially bid you adieu, how
she died at sixty-four, and when I cleaned
out her drawers, I found her diaphragm
intact, though her periods stopped
with the chemo in her forties.

You assumed I'd join the ranks
of my friends who'd chosen
single motherhood with sperm donors
in their thirties. In my forties,
you disapproved when I told
my new husband I'd never
have children with him
because of the schizophrenia
in his tree. I stand by that.
I suspect you had valid reasons,
though my nutritionist simply blamed
your tenacity on cows, made me go cold
turkey on dairy. It didn't help.
But I miss you now. And Dr. D.'s attention,
how she marveled each time she drew blood.

Ultima Thule: New Year's Day 2019

As the books closed like a welcome
mat on a year of disquiet
writ rackety in the world,
writ rankling in my own grief,
the New Horizons spacecraft skirted
an ancient space rock four billion
miles away, a billion beyond Pluto.

Like a lead apron that repels
radiating assaults, I'd deflected
earthly things for months, gave up
committee meetings and cable news
to offer leavened breads, unleavened
truths, soggy tissues, and bad poetry
as sacrifices for my sins,
as offerings for my contrition.

Humbled when Ultima Thule's
images were beamed back
from a far-flung system,
I parachuted to virgin ground,
a golden dandelion turned pappus.

Taking root, my inner new year stood
on the sidelines of outer space to welcome
its vastness: *How great are Your works,
Eternal One; how deep Your designs.*

Ultima Thule, *a place beyond the known,*
was a divine secret and hiding place for God,
for Whom billions of years and miles
are just a flash and a yardstick.

Tainted by Nazi myth, her name
was re-christened *sky*
in the language of the Powhatan—
Arrokoth. And if I dare look up
in wonder, I test my own arrogance
as to what I can see every day
against the unknown known.

3

Starter Mothers

About 87 miles southeast of Brussels, the residents of a living
library are fermenting away.
—Smithsonianmag.com

They come to Sankt Vith from Peru
and Malta, Japan, and the States
for safekeeping, speaking a language
that bubbles up as a beige glob
of bacteria when flour meets water.
Unlike me, they are mothers, all
125 of them, catalogued and shelved,
refrigerated and honored. They are fed
every two months from a reserve
of flour bequeathed by their bakers
for perpetual care. A mother
from Greece is kept alive by holy water
infused with basil. A Swiss mother
has discovered a long-lost cousin
from Mexico—they share the same wild
Torulaspora present in none
of the others. Blame it on the altitude,
or on a universal Venn diagram
that connects everything. I recognize
the lust for immortality.

Some claim to be centuries old,
but who's to say for sure.
Their aim is self-perpetuation,
these starters, and their history
is baked into exodus tales
the world over, carried as family
heirlooms over passes and oceans.
Fortune seekers carried flour
and mother from the Arctic
north, became fabled gold miners
cuddling San Francisco sourdoughs
on cold nights to keep them warm.

I myself have felt the burden
of such a mother. *It's hard
to kill her,* my friend said
when I forgot to feed the one
she'd gifted me.

Which of those mothers,
despite their joie de vivre,
hasn't at times thought to end
it all rather than be dissected
and probed for microbes
and medieval secrets
in that library of forever?

I know mother lust
and death lust, too,
like unfermented dust,
sterile dreams of wheat rot
in my mouth, sour and raw.

Cousin J.

We all knew she kept the Angel
of Death on speed-dial for a face-
to-face over chamomile tea laced
with pills she'd squirreled away.

A stone-deaf woman in her 90's,
she had important things to think
about in her vaulted hush.
She'd been around the block,

was nothing if not pragmatic:
I've had much, I don't need more.
Her men had all emptied the linty
pockets of her heart: her husband,

her firstborn, my brother,
both her brothers, and Hurricane
Harvey—all in short order.
She interrogated the dirt and the blood

and the likelihood of diapers to come.
She enlisted a ministering
angel, a friend, to ferry her across
the border with no fuss, no mess,

leaving us—a cadre of admirers—
golden nuggets and salty tissues
from her pockets, and a hush in which
to ponder important and messy things.

Being Woman as Superpower

When my niece asked, *If you could fly*
or be invisible, which would you choose?
I said, *Fly*, because I'm a woman
and had already been gifted the other without ever asking.

Like that time I waited in line at Sears to return
a busted garden hose while the genial salesman—
let's call him Gene—helped a woman
whose hearing aid screeched
return a microwave from another state
with a different sales tax, and then
a shy pre-teen boy with pimples
earnestly inquired about the camping gear
he might need for the White Mountains.
Gene saw me, knew I was waiting
as any decent person would until the boy
walked away with his annotated shopping list,
when this guy in a suit and a swagger strode
to the counter clamoring for a lawnmower.
Gene pointed in the general direction, turned
to me apologetically, but the suit said,
In five minutes I leave here
with a good mower and a warranty.
Gene, unable to distinguish an imminent
from a slow-building volcano, made his choice.
What am I, chopped liver? I yelled,
following after, this woman whose forbearance
would not abide cutting the queue. Stalking them,
I learned the pros and cons of self-propelled
versus electric. *Admit it, if I'd been a man,*
you wouldn't do this, disgusting
myself by naming the conspiracy.
I left with my new hose,
and the name of Gene's supervisor.

I've been overlooked at least 3,333 times
when my genitalia proved insufficient
to bear my proper title, Rabbi. Invisibility
is a superpower desired by the young,
the crooked, or the shamed. But I, who come by it
naturally, would exchange it for just one chance
to enter again that synagogue that refused
to count me, so I might recite the mourners' prayer
for the still essential, yet invisible brother of mine.
So, I said to my niece, *Invisibility*
is over-rated. Let's try shapeshifting.

Bird in Captivity

Be like the bird who pausing in her flight awhile on boughs
too slight feels them give way beneath her,
yet sings, knowing she has wings.
    —*Victor Hugo*

You were shooting hoops in the driveway
with your twelve-year-old son.

This was a dream he had
after you died.

He left you outside, went in the house,
not sure why,

but when he came back
you were a bird,

all pin feathers, ebbing to silence,
heading south across the sky.

The Little Prince Said It First

What is essential is invisible to the eye—
knowing this to be true, troubled
by what I saw straight-on
and sideways in my periphery,
I set my eyes on building heaven
on earth, as naive, some thought,

as that golden-curled space
traveler with his signature scarf.
By then I had words for *calling*
and *sacred*, for *glory* and *grace*,
and for the animal spirit galloping
in me, its invitation to wrangle

clouds into patterns of meaning,
ride dolphins bareback into town,
defender of children and other living
things, and to lie belly-up
like a cat, exposed, because students
want to see how the rabbi ties her shoes.

I trained to spelunk in caves
of the heart, certain of the patience
of bulbs below ground. I sniffed hard-
to-reach blessings in crevices
of human grief, even when miles
and months away, like a polar bear

on the scent of a seal three feet
under ice. By then I knew synesthesia
was a paradox of spiritual
wholeness, like John Locke's
blind man who smelled the color
scarlet when he heard a trumpet blast.

I, too, touch and taste red when the alarm
rouses me to the world ablaze,
the Garden distant. That's when I miss
my mother and think of the rose
alone in the bell jar, the one
we're all called to raise.

The Angel Came to You as Picasso
—for Ellen

> Every child is an artist. The problem is how to remain an artist
> once he grows up.
> —Pablo Picasso

The philtrum just above your upper lip
where a finger fits so perfectly, any finger,
but, let's say, one on your left hand,

your painter's hand, the one that divulges
holy secrets on canvas—it was sculpted,
so goes the legend, by the angel Lailah

when you were born, that groove
in your face, in mine, in anyone's.
In the womb she taught you caverns

within caverns of Torah by the glow
of a candle that let you view all worlds
in every dimension, past and coming.

She held a mirror to your face, acquainting
you with splendor. You might have been born
haloed yourself, had she not tapped you

there with her own slender finger,
so you forgot everything but the desire
for all she'd stolen, a suspicion

that followed you like an echo.
So when you told me your dream,
the one where Picasso taught you

all he knew about art and laying brush
to palette—though you call it a visit,
even recalling the weight

and voice of him—and how fifty years later,
you're still recovering
all he revealed, I thought of Lailah

and how we spend our lives
tracking those kaleidoscope truths
she'd imparted *in utero*

telescoping back and forward, filaments
of light and color, as crumbs and whispers
on the scavenger hunt of our lives.

Wreaking Havoc, Newark, 1921, Ad Nauseam

My father manspreads, knowing he is to be the last of four
to kick around in my grandmother's womb
now that she's heard Margaret Sanger's gospel
in Brooklyn and protects herself with a diaphragm
when my grandfather comes to her lunchtimes from the store.

No need to make it easier on her, his unnatural mother,
who wishes she'd met that woman rebel two pregnancies
ago. He kicks hard, leaves her nauseous every morning.
Already he relishes the havoc he will inflict to test her
limits, not imagining he'll grow bored of the drinking

boys and hussies by 37, and want to settle down
with a nice Jewish girl who also protects herself
(with his permission) and have three kids—two girls
well-spaced, the youngest, a boy, unexpected,
whose own breaches he can barely abide—or that he'll buy

out his father's hardware store with his brother and stand
long hours shooting stale breeze with his customers,
charming housewives and swapping salty jokes with men
in splotched work boots and overalls. He couldn't have known
how I, his oldest, would be imprinted by those uniforms,

men who plumb and paint, hammer and saw, marrying one
of my own—a shop teacher, good with his hands—
long after my father had joined his mother in perpetuity
at King Solomon Cemetery, or how Margaret would emboss
my rebel soul, poised to vent havoc on his world.

A New Song

Where have all the flowers gone?
—*Pete Seeger*

Before the Hallowed Return
the Great Howl swallowed
Small Hope's song.   His roar
stole all breath of her
melody   silenced all relic
of her desire.   He swept ice floes
in the North into sandstorms swirling
in the South   and back
again.   Eons begat eons.   Dervishes
of scorching tumult and arctic
rumble hovered over the Crater
of the Deep   the Howl's
          henchmen   vigilant.

Small Hope kept singing   *Arise.*
You're not alone. Arise   arise!
trying to score purchase
within the piercing cacophony
of the Howl.   From Ice
to Desert Age   over and again
she sang until   from both East
and West   the ice thawed
into dew   the temperate dawn of Flora
verdant   despite the roar
          a first day.

After the algae   moss.   After fern
fungi   gingko   conifer   fig.
After croci   honeysuckle   wafting
in the flow of the Great Howl
who paused   a ripple   pleasure
perhaps   imperceptible
          a second day.

Small Hope's song caught his sharp
inhale   flung   *Not alone   Arise!*
to echo into the ether on her own
breath.   Her voice roused
the sleeping   the departed
and the yet-to-be from the Crater
of the Deep   animated

all castaways in their crypts
            a third day.

Creatures winged   legged   finned
headed home to air   to land
to sea and stream   soaring
scampering   splashing
Alive   Alive
            a fourth day.

Small Hope birthed
Big Dreams each day.
Back to the wheat   the Baker.
To the flax   the Seamstress
the Builder   to the straw
the Dancer   to the sky
the Poet   to the wind.
She seeded the Hallowed Return
a Sabbath of Rejoicing   a new song
fledged from
            the hollows   again.

Over the Ocean

At the doorway to the hospital room,
high above southbound traffic
on Lexington, I catch live coverage
of Mandela's release from Robben Island,
Winnie and Nelson hand-in-hand, cheered,
waving. I, chaplain on call, turn
towards the bed to celebrate history
in the making. The woman's eyes
seek mine. Her breath pads
lightly, like a cat kneading,
pawing, sweat sprinkled salty
on her upper lip. Low in her chest,
a gurgle. I squeeze her hand,
and with my other, press
the button for the nurse, grab
a tissue to dab her forehead
and neck. Her green eyes begin
to glaze. I remember she has no
family here, think of her Irish lilt.
Her name, *Bonnie*. I can't summon
that blessing, the one about the road
rising, the wind at your back.
I sing instead. *My Bonnie lies
over the ocean…Oh, bring back
my Bonnie to me.* The TV streams
dancing in Capetown, the trilling
crowds jostling their moving car.
Two nurses fiddle with machines
and measurements, glossy white
cords governing life and death. *You look
like a deer in the headlights*, one says.
Your first? I shake my head *no*, as I remember
singing my mother across, singing
to keep terror confined on an island
with no ferryman or bridge to span.

And Sora Laughed

"It was a small town, so our meshugener was only half-crazy."
—Jonathan Boyarin, ed., A Ruined Garden:
The Memorial Books of Polish Jewry

Crazy Sora walks the streets
of shtetl-town begging food
for her armful of rags   her phantom baby
        Just a nosh so he can sleep tonight

We give some *zlotys*   a *knish* or two
so Sora can sleep
        so we can too

Sometimes she appraises the proffered hand
predicts a windfall   a straying husband
the end of the world
prophesies   *God is glass*
The sky is shedding
        shards of Him

When the Schutzstaffel comes,
she walks among the chosen
Left   they bark
upon seeing the rumpled nomad
mumble to herself   cradling
        an armful of rags

They prod her privates
spit *Schmutziger Jew*
She flings a colorful string
of Yiddish curses from all of us
in return   *May you crap*
blood and pus   marry
the daughter of the Angel
of Death   hang by day and burn
        by night like a chandelier

cooing and rocking her make-believe
child in her *meshugener* way
before laying her bundle atop our troves
sepia snapshots   silver candlesticks
        pillows of down

Meshugener Sora is carted away with the elders

Meshugener Sora laughs
when she realizes what an artful trick
she has played   She laughs all
the way to camp   all the way
    to the showers

But the nozzles don't work
the stall is clogged by bodies
arms and breasts
    She hears footsteps on the ceiling

We scream blood and murder
                        geischrei gevalt
while she claws her laughter   the laughter
we used to join   into the cement walls
        her fetus cackling itself to sleep

Too late to wish her luck
beneath an auspicious constellation—
Mazel tov—though billions of years
after conception

                        even a dying star

        has matter

The Hostess

The spider assesses the angles of the rafters
from her recessed nook. She lifts an appendage,

ready to prepare a bed for her expected guest.
Her life depends on his arrival, be it by wing or leg.

She extrudes the most viscous thread of silk she can
muster from a spinneret at the tip of her abdomen

so her visitor can't slide from his sloped berth.
That first silky strand drifts on a faint breeze until

it fastens to a surface some distance from where she
is perched. She reels in the filament, tensing it,

and gingerly walks its length with a second strand
in tow, trading two pairs of legs in the air, two

on the tightrope, the hairs on her feet offering grip
whether she is upside-down or sideways.

She repeats until this suspended bridge
supports the rest of the guest room. She spins

out radials before fortifying the center into a spiral
orb of geometric genius. What she expends

in energy now, she expects her guest to repay.
She is nothing if not frugal. When he fails

to appear by daybreak, she consumes the web to recoup
her strength and begins again. When he later lands

at his lodgings, fluttering, she welcomes him
venomously. Despite his protests, she divines

his exhaustion, indifferent to her own. Casting another
glutinous thread, she swaddles him until his wings

still, and his many eyes are blinded to her efforts.
She dines alone, refusing to disturb her company

from his repose, while downstairs, humming,
I make the bed for my own guest, a stew
just beginning to bubble on the stove.

Conjuring Bread from Earth
for Rob

...at the still point, there the dance is.
—*T.S. Eliot*

There you are, baking bread
before sunrise, a masseuse kneading
its knots and sinews. You divine
the dough's perfect balance
between a big-belly Buddha
and a contortionist, nudging
it to stretch and   elasticize,
while willing it to find
its enlightened self at rest,
brooding its next incarnation,
      as light slyly crawls,
            then leaps across the room
like Degas' dancer from her pose.

Eve Shelters in Place

What more could I have wanted than this gift of ample time
to shelter with my beloved, the one with the upper-case B,
and the human one sharing my bed. Runaways from the Babel

of the urban Apple to this paradise of tempo-lento, we inhabit
our garden alone. It's overgrown like my hair, wild, satiated
by Eden's cukes and kale, our bodies and my spirit toned

by prayer and passion. Ripened through daily devotion, all
we need seems right here, in the blessing of body, with breath
that blows through the cage of ribs and tingles my kissed skin.

It is what I hold in the palm of my hand—that wildflower
Blake taught is heaven, that grain of sand bearing the world.
But I am shamed by this pleasure, this Eden as refuge

as I chew on the naked gospel of the world, this Hobson's choice
I made in this parade of trees, a flaming sword en garde, taunting.

Elegy for the Lady on Liberty Island

> *A mighty woman with a torch, whose flame*
> *Is the imprisoned lightning, and her name*
> *Mother of Exiles.*
>> —*Emma Lazarus, "The New Colossus"*

Curse that raised torch, quivering lips, the broken chain
and shackles as good as whole at her feet, girding
her womb. She wears the blue patina of sorrow, pregnant
with dreams of home across the sea, *parlez-vous?*,
and nowhere to go but a back alley in Queens, women
crossing borders from Ohio and Missouri, frenzied escape
from a fate that biology conferred. While hope scrambles
for a foothold on slippery benches of high courts,
she extends her arm to the sky. Damn the pedestal
on which she stands—ironic welcome to foreigners
who come now by foot or air, rarely by sea, and a virgin/
whore two-punch to those who hold up half the sky. Damn
the sonnet that Emma wrote that raised the funds
that raised that pedestal on which she stands, branding
her *Mother*. She would suckle all comers who want to breathe
free, but instead coughs and gasps, herself bound by symbolic
satire. Let's raise Cain and eyebrows, unplucked,
bushy, link arms, chant, *This is what it looks like,*
kindle the torch until we are hoarse, until she is no lady.

Dropping Stones from the Heart

Take your right hand, palm open,
elbow bent, and slap your heart
for each of the six days of Creation.
On the seventh beat, drop your arm
to nest at your side, fingertips
brushing your hip. Like a silk scarf
swan, flutter to stillness,

breathe sabbath. Repeat seven beats,
seven times, as time deepens into time,
moments wax and wane into new
moons and full. Count the Omer,
sabbatical years and jubilee,
eons and ages, Ice and Bronze,
Iron Age, New Age, Wise Age.

Confess and pound your chest
closed-fisted on Atonement Day,
recall things past where you have erred
as baldly as air, as heedlessly
as a brimming tub of water.

Pound then drop, pound
then drop the stones you've lugged,
skeletons collecting dust in the jammed
attic of your scruples, rent-free.

You've always held the code
to redemption, like ruby slippers
spiraling you back and forward to Eden,
summer falling into winter,
and springing you from jail.

Massage your heart
open, wriggle your way
toward a grace
as surprising as lavender
crocuses piercing icy ground.

After all the weighty lifting, freight
self-inflicted, tap your heels, brush
your leg with an olive branch,
embrace the tiger, tamed
and free, teeth bared.

Neverland

We giggled through all seasons:
camping in the cabin out back,
heaps of leaves rolling out the red
carpet for our falls, snow angels,
wings and legs flapping. Inside,
we three tip-toed around
our mother's blues and seizures,
modeled her lingerie and high
heels, morphed ourselves into shapes
equilateral, obtuse, or acute,
depending on the day's allegiances.

Long after we Wendy Darlings
traded freedom for duty,
our brother still wished upon
the star of happily-afters.
He stayed clear of rostrums,
dogfights, and pirates. He dressed
in skeleton leaves handed down
from our parents, an outfit
which crumbled inexorably, fleck
by fleck, until he was naked
and flying, trailing magic
duff and eggshells in his wake
for as far as we could see.

The Time Turner, as Seen on Facebook

You would have bought it, too,
Potter fan, had it popped up
on your Facebook feed
for the mere price of shipping—
a gaudy knock-off of Hermione's pendant,
the one she used to travel time.

I sobbed as I tapped my name,
address, credit card number
into the appropriate fields,
and clicked *Confirm*.

I knew it was a fiction,
but I bought it anyway, because
I wanted magic, miracle,
a maneuver to reverse what's unfolded,
and offer my brother a chance
to stand again on that bridge
from which he'd jumped,
and turn—his children still
in bed—walk the twenty feet
back to his car, and drive home.

The Royal We

The queen bee lays between 1,000 and 2,000 eggs a day…
If the queen bee fertilizes the egg, that egg will become female.
—*sciencing.com*

Your lot may want to stay clear of the nest,
but mine clamor for closeness, can't do
enough to wait on me—by wing and corbiculae—
all 60,000 plus of them. They flutter and flap
if it's hot, flap and flutter when it's cold.
Their lifting off and landing is a constant buzzsaw
gnawing at that oak outside. I'm deadly sick
of this throne existence—pampered and plumped—
not even in charge of my own waste. Oh, here
she comes, my jack-of-all-trades, one of my many,
disposing of my crap with a rear leg while feeding
me royal jelly with a front. Repulsive, really. Most days,
I revel in reliving my maiden flight. They would die for me,
those boys, so mad to mate. I strung them
along for their millions, sperm stored now
for a lifetime. I dole it out bit by bit for my girls,
who grow up to think me just a handmaid, born
to breed more of them in my image. But to be
or not be female, I choose for them with a flick
of my spermatheca. A scant privilege of royalty,
sweet and sticky like revenge.

Capricorn Loses His Star

The goat will carry on itself all their sins to a solitary place.
—Leviticus 16:22

May you have a good constellation,
mazal tov, the stars aligned
in your favor. But the he-goat trills

in tragedy, while we dance circles
around him, blood in our eyes,
sneering at his bad luck. Tragedy

is the song we sing around the altar
of his sacrifice. Or perhaps the goat
is the prize for our singing, and he

doesn't die at all. The Greek
is ambiguous, and it's a holy day
of reckoning and catharsis in the Bible,

for which he's kept our accounts square
for over five thousand years, his life
breaking-even against ours. For him

(he-goat, sea-goat, scapegoat), it's inevitable—
losing his bearings, his compass, his hitch
to a star. He is synonymous with falls,

meteoric, with staged calamity—
satyrs singing odes to the gods.
Four kinds of tragedy: complicated,

simple, moral and the one about losing
a star—disastrous—poetic
as the naming of the four children

at the seder, wise and wicked,
simple, and silent, and that kid
in the song bought for two *zuzim*,

a happy ending until the cat showed up
and devoured it. When our goat loses
his star, we lose our desire for the sea

to which he's bound. But still we rise
to the occasion, our hooves scaling
the mountainside, our hands to the sky.

With Thanks

Special thanks to my husband, dear friends, relatives and the many fantastic poets and teachers who have guided and honored my writing journey. My brother Howard is ever my muse. As I work and re-work my poems, Travis Denton has served faithfully and patiently as poetry guru, cheerleader, editor, and friend. I am blessed.

Pamela **Wax** is the author of *Walking the Labyrinth* (Main Street Rag, 2022), a finalist for MSR's poetry book contest. Her poems have received awards and commendations from *Crosswinds, Paterson Literary Review, Nimrod, Poets' Billow, Oberon, Solstice,* and the Robinson Jeffers Tor House, as well as a Best of the Net nomination, and have appeared in journals including *Barrow Street, Tupelo Quarterly, About Place Journal, Rust & Moth, Mudfish, Connecticut River Review, Naugatuck River Review, Pedestal, Split Rock Review, Slippery Elm, Sixfold,* and *Passengers Journal.* Wax is an ordained rabbi, pastoral counselor, and sought-after teacher, who leads on-line spirituality workshops, including poetry writing, and travels around the country as scholar/artist-in-residence. Her essays on Judaism, spirituality, and women's issues have also been published broadly. She walks labyrinths in the Northern Berkshires of Massachusetts, or wherever she can find them.

www.ingramcontent.com/pod-product-compliance
Lightning Source LLC
Chambersburg PA
CBHW022045080426
42734CB00009B/1252